BRANDING:
Distilled

A GUIDE TO PACKAGE DESIGN FOR CRAFT SPIRITS

CYNTHIA STERLING

Published by White Mule Press,
a division of the American Distilling Institute™

© 2015 Sterling Creativeworks
sterlingcreativeworks.com
All rights reserved.

Printed in the United States of America.

ISBN 978-0-9910436-7-5

whitemulepress.com
cheers@whitemulepress.com
PO Box 577
Hayward, CA 94541 -USA

TABLE OF CONTENTS

FOREWORD
JAMES RODEWALD

In 1998, on a trip to Portland, Oregon, I walked into Clear Creek Distillery and met the owner, Stephen McCarthy. At the time I had been working at *Gourmet* magazine for a few months, but I was still several years away from becoming its drinks editor. And, like most people in the days before the resurrection of cocktail culture, which brought increased attention to booze quality, I was more focused on wine than spirits. But I'd never seen the inside of a distillery, and I was curious.

As I tasted through McCarthy's eaux de vie, grappa and what was at the time America's only single malt, curiosity turned to fascination and a seed was planted. It took 15 years, but that seed eventually grew into my recent book on craft distillers, *American Spirit: An Exploration of the Craft Distilling Revolution.* The explosive growth in the number of small, independent distilleries in the intervening years is nothing short of incredible—from fewer than 40 distilleries in 1998, to more than 600 in 2014—and the book you now hold in your hands is additional proof that the category is more than a niche, more than a novelty: it's a full-fledged business. That's why an examination of the importance of branding to success in craft spirits is so timely.

That day at Clear Creek I sampled five of the seven products the distillery was making; today the company (which McCarthy sold to Hood River Distillers in 2014) produces nearly two dozen. The idea that a small American company with no marketing budget, no sales force and a product with almost no following could expect to still be in business 15 years later, let alone be the target of a buyout, would have struck me as absurdly far-fetched in 1998. That McCarthy had been in business at that point for more than 10 years struck me at the time as entirely a testament to one man's drive, commitment and distilling talent. At least in part, what made it possible to actually grow the business, hire a part-time bookkeeper, a couple of salespeople and a distillery manager was the rapidly rising tide of craft spirits in general. Many consumers want to be on the cutting edge, but very few are willing to be the only ones making the leap. So even more than the resurgence of interest in cocktails, early craft distillers like Clear Creek probably benefited from the large second wave of small, independent spirits producers whose creations began to hit liquor store shelves and back bars in the early 2000s.

Another big moment in my professional imbibing career came in 2004. While looking for special bottles for the gift guide for the December issue of *Gourmet*, I came across a Germain-Robin brandy made entirely from Pinot Noir grapes. I was floored. By then I'd been lucky enough to taste some pretty great brandies, including Cognacs made from wines distilled in the 1800s, but I fell in love with that American-made (though by the capable French hands of Hubert Germain-Robin, of course) spirit. I was starting to get the impression that this country was capable of making more than just big, bold bourbons (not that there's anything wrong with that). It was around this time that a few breweries began distilling tiny batches of various experimental fermentations. In a matter of just a few years, the craft spirits landscape (not that there was such a category, yet) had gone from a handful of very committed, extremely talented, slowly-going-broke craftsmen to several hundred distillers of varying shapes, sizes and abilities.

And thank goodness. If Clear Creek and Germain-Robin—not to mention St. George, Osocalis, Anchor Distilling and Tuthilltown—had not paved the way, and if all the creative, driven and fearless men and women hadn't followed in their footsteps, I wouldn't have had much to write about. In the course of researching and writing *American Spirit*, two things came up time and time again: authenticity and transparency. In the short time since my book was published there have been a few class-action lawsuits targeting misleading labeling by spirits producers. Is there a surer sign of the maturing of an American industry than parades of lawyers? Nearly every distiller I interviewed who was actually making what they were selling expressed frustration with those who were buying and bottling and trying to make it seem as if they were, in fact, distilling their products. It didn't take long for me to come to the conclusion that one of the main advantages—and perhaps the only one—that small, independent producers have over their larger counterparts is transparency. If you're making whiskey in a pot still, using grain from a local farmer, doing everything yourself, you can, and probably should, brag about it. You can't compete for placement on liquor store shelves with brands who can pay for increased visibility, you can't afford to send out an army of "brand ambassadors" to give away gallons of your product, but you can tell the truth.

Given the increasing numbers of bottles and labels popping up on shelves from coast to coast, it's now more necessary than ever to catch a potential customer's eye. It's often said of packaging that you have to grab a consumer's attention in 10 seconds or less, but I'm not sure that's necessarily true when it comes to high-end spirits. Thoughtful spirits lovers seem more likely than most to at least spin that bottle around. I've certainly observed shoppers reading every word on dozens of labels trying to figure out which bottle to buy, but that's obviously the exception. So yes, eye-grabbing graphics are important—that first sale is always the hardest to make—but I think it's even more important to communicate who you are and what you stand for. A critical element of that is branding, and as we move toward the inevitable shake-out in the industry, the only thing that's nearly as important as what's *in* the bottle is what's *on* the bottle. And the best way to learn how to do that is...turn the page.

The craft spirits category is young, thriving and growing at a phenomenal pace. The diversity and style of craft spirits packaging is a delight for spirits lovers and design lovers alike, offering a feast for the eyes as well as for the palate. However, if the growth model of the wine and craft beer categories holds true for spirits, we'll eventually see some brands rise to the top and become iconic, while others languish in obscurity.

As the shelves become more crowded, the importance of a thoughtful, strategic approach to brand development cannot be overstated. Good product quality is necessary for a brand's reputation to take hold, but strong branding and packaging are keys to getting people to try your product in the first place. They provide the vehicle that will give your brand momentum and longevity.

We've selected packages from across the country to showcase here. While we hope to provide visual inspiration to lovers of craft spirits, our aim is to offer insight into best practices for branding and design so that distillers and other specialty producers can use this book as a resource to gain an edge in the marketplace and bring their product to a larger audience.

WHAT IS BRANDING?

A brand is more than a logo or a label. Marketer and author, Seth Godin, defines a brand as "the set of expectations, memories, stories and relationships that, taken together, account for a consumer's decision to choose one product or service over another." People buy brands, and then share them, based upon their emotional response to what they see and hear. Yes, the product quality matters, but studies have shown that even the customer's flavor experience is strongly influenced by the package design.

Branding is the strategic process by which we uncover and develop this deeper story, draw out its unique emotional appeal, and then express it through the brand name and package design. Branding includes the verbal and visual expression of the distiller's story and every aspect of the brand's identity in the marketplace, from the bottle to the website.

DISTILLERY   BEEHIVE DISTILLING
PACKAGE DESIGN   In-house

BRANDING STARTS WITH STRATEGY

Branding, when done well, starts with a deep exploration of the story of the people, production process and idea behind your product. The distillers, distributors and retailers we interviewed for this book consistently mentioned the importance of a well-expressed, authentic story. People seek an emotional connection to the brands they purchase, and this drives their willingness to pay a premium for a distilled spirit. A compelling story is what motivates retailers, and ultimately consumers, to select one brand over another.

Your unique brand story answers the questions of why your product exists, why it is special, and why people should care. It expresses the big idea behind your product, and answers the questions about how and by whom it's made, what ingredients and care go into it, and where it's from. It's memorable, relatable, compelling and always ties back to the product itself. Your brand name should embody this big idea, and the visual expression of that idea becomes the basis for your package design.

A PACKAGE IS ABOUT MORE THAN AESTHETICS

Good packaging design is an aesthetic delight, and, as designers ourselves, we are easily seduced by style, detail and imagery for its own sake. What makes a package great, however, goes far beyond pure aesthetics. Packaging has a job to do—in many cases it is the only communication vehicle your brand has, and must make the sale without any additional information.

A great package should fit its category but also stand out within it. It should grab the eye from the retail shelf and the back bar. And once it has captured attention, it must convey the essence of the brand and invite the viewer to explore more deeply. It must express the brand's personality, and deliver the key reasons to believe.

As the craft spirits category becomes more crowded, branding takes on new and growing importance. The case studies, articles and images in this book showcase a broad range of styles and approaches. They may provide a strategic model and inspiration, but ultimately each brand needs to find its own authentic visual and verbal voice. We hope you'll use this book to discover the tools and resources to create your own unique identity.

THE ANATOMY OF PACKAGE DESIGN

A — Brand Logotype

Your brand name and its typographic treatment convey your brand's unique character. Make sure the brand name is large enough to read from a back bar, contrasts well with the background color, and that the letterforms are easy to decipher. No matter how recognizable your label or bottle is, your brand name must be easy to recall and easy to say, so that consumers are comfortable asking for it.

B — Label Shape

A unique label shape helps your package stand out and be memorable. This is especially important when using a stock bottle shape.

C — Closure

The closure is an opportunity to reinforce branding and convey product quality. Attention to detail here pays off, since the end user will handle this part of your package each time they open the bottle.

D — Neck Label

Whether wrapped over the closure vertically or applied around the neck, a neck label conveys the distiller's attention to detail. It's a good place to add secondary messaging without cluttering the face label. The neck label can be used to color code different product types within the line.

E — Bottle Shape

Your bottle shape is the first thing noticed and should fit the product category while also being as distinctive as possible within it. Visualize the brands you know well, and notice how key the bottle shape is to recalling the package.

F — Illustration or Icon

A custom illustration or graphic symbol visually expresses your brand story. It also works as an identifier when describing the brand, and is especially useful when the name is hard to recall.

G — Romance or Descriptive Copy

A few key words that describe the unique qualities of your product or tell your brand story can be a powerful addition to the front panel, so long as they don't interfere with the readability and impact of the brand logo and other critical information.

H — Product Type

The prominence of the product type can vary depending on how many SKUs are in your line. It should be secondary to the brand name. Consumers and bartenders need to identify what is in the bottle, but this information should not override the brand name or visual story.

I — Legal Copy

The TTB regulates the size and position of alcohol content and volume. See Chapter 10 for more information about compliance and the approval process for labels.

Back Panel (not pictured)

Once your front panel and bottle shape have enticed a consumer to pick up your bottle, the back panel copy is your opportunity to tell them more about your product and story. Don't skimp on copywriting — the content and the tone of voice used here are a big part of your brand's expression.

A

B

C

D

E

F

G

H

I

A good design partner will help you clarify your brand vision, and then bring it into tangible form. Unfortunately, few startup distillers have experience finding a design partner and managing the design process. An understanding of the branding process will help you research and evaluate design professionals to find the right fit, and help ensure that you enter the market with a strong, strategically sound brand design.

SELECTING A PRO

Selecting the right branding and design team involves more than looking at portfolios. Whether you choose to work with a solo freelance designer or an established design firm, make sure they are experienced in branding and packaging design, and make sure that their approach to design is based on a sound strategic development process.

There are many designers with attractive portfolios full of engaging design work. Brand owners are often seduced by style, and although this is one important consideration, it's at least as important that you like the way they think and solve problems. This is hard to assess simply by looking at their work.

Talk with designers you are considering, and listen to how they describe their process. How and why did they arrive at each design solution they show you? They should talk about communicating the key messages to the target audience, and how the design they developed does this. Hearing how they think, looking at their work, and making sure they understand your vision are the three keys to making a good choice.

WORKING THROUGH THE PROCESS

Good design develops over phases. The initial phase should be focused on understanding the brand's essence, its key messages, the motivation of the target audience and the visual solutions that will engage them emotionally. This is what we call design strategy. A strategic approach to branding delivers design that not only looks great, but also does its intended job well—selling your brand even when you are not there to tell your story.

-BRIEF-

⋮

DISCOVERY & ANALYSIS

⋮

{1}

DELIVER:
DESIGN STRATEGY
MOOD BOARD
BRAND ESSENCE
NAMING

⋮

DESIGN & DEVELOP ·······▶

{2}

DELIVER:
BRAND STORY
PACKAGE CONCEPTS
GLASS DESIGN

·······▶

REFINE & VALIDATE ·······▶

PHASE 1: DISCOVERY AND ANALYSIS

This first phase begins with information gathering. The goal is to develop a deep understanding of a brand owner's objectives. The design team immerses themselves in the brand's competitive set, consumers, retail environment and vision. This critical knowledge forms the foundation of a comprehensive design exploration.

PHASE 2: DESIGN DEVELOPMENT

From this foundation, a range of visual design ideas is developed. These design concepts are presented for evaluation along with the rationale for each. The number of options varies greatly by firm. At the end of Phase 2, one or more designs should be selected for refinement.

PHASES 3 & 4: DESIGN REFINEMENT AND COMPREHENSIVES

The selected design(s) are refined. Back panel design is completed, and all elements are presented for approval. If budget allows, a mock-up or tight comprehensive, showing all the elements in 3D form may be provided for final approval.

PHASE 5: PRODUCTION & IMPLEMENTATION:

Proper execution of the design is essential. Your design firm should meet with the printers and fabricators to establish specifications that maximize your production budget and deliver the best appearance on the shelf. They will then prepare the design for final reproduction. The final files, with specifications, will be provided to you for proofing and approval—make sure you take the time to review carefully. Your design team should also provide production management for the finished project, including attending a press check during the print runs of the various packaging components.

With the right creative team, a clear process and good communication, the development of your brand identity can be one of the most exciting and rewarding steps in launching your product. Most people have the mistaken notion that great design comes from talent or a stroke of inspiration. In reality, great design is the result of a clear strategy and a well-managed process. Only with these two things in place can we focus our creativity on designing a compelling package that grabs the eye of consumers and captures their hearts, turning a curious prospect into a loyal fan and champion for your brand.

{5}

ASSESS:
REVIEW RESULTS
DEVELOP MARKETING
TOOLS

↑

[**LAUNCH**]

↑

{3}

DELIVER:
REFINED STORY
REFINED PACKAGING

· · · · · · ·> [**IMPLEMENT**] · · · · · · ·>

{4}

DELIVER:
MECHANICAL ART
PRINT SUPERVISION
POS CONCEPTS

SPIRIT WORKS DISTILLERY

FOUNDER	Timo and Ashby Marshall
EST. 2013	SPIRITS GIN, VODKA, WHISKEY
LOCATION	Sebastopol, California
PACKAGE DESIGN	Ingalls Design

Husband and wife team Timo and Ashby Marshall wanted to move from San Francisco to Sonoma County, to buy land and grow botanicals for gin and sloe gin. Originally, they intended to find an existing craft distillery to collaborate in their gin-making vision, but came up empty handed. As they researched, they fell in love with the idea of doing their own distilling and instead built Spirit Works, in Sebastopol, California.

What inspired you to start a distillery?

In England it's common for people who live in the countryside to make sloe gin by macerating sloe berries in gin. It's enjoyed as a digestif after dinner, and there is a lot of family pride in the quality of their homemade sloe gin. My family has made it for generations in the UK, using sloes handpicked every autumn along the coastal hills. Ashby and I wanted to make the same homemade quality here.

We were looking for a grain to glass distillery in Northern California we could partner with, but couldn't find one. This led us to think about building our own distillery, and we got hooked. We put our vision of buying land on hold and went for it.

What products do you make?

We make everything here by hand at the distillery—grain to glass. We make our base spirit, which is our vodka, which then becomes our gin. We make a traditional sloe gin and a barrel-aged gin. We are also currently barrel-aging both a straight wheat whiskey and a straight rye whiskey. We're always experimenting, trying new things.

Timo and Ashby Marshall of Spirit Works Distillery

How did you come up with your brand name and what is the meaning behind it?

We spent a fair amount of time developing our name. We wanted to convey that we are actual producers. We liked the word "works," as in an industrial steel works, because it conveys the work of producing something. Spirit Works was the name commonly used for distilleries before the word distillery came into use in Europe. Ashby and I worked on the naming ourselves. We wanted to have ownership of the process. It involved lots of brainstorming and the drinking of lots of gin and tonics.

Tell us about your journey from the idea of launching a spirits brand to the actual launch.

It took us about five years from the idea to launch. Most of that time was spent going back to school to learn about distilling and running a business. Everything from milling grain to accounting. We left our previous jobs about two years before the product was ready to sell to work full time on the distillery.

Once you had a brand name, how did you find a designer to help with branding and packaging design?

We approached many designers who never replied back because we were a startup. We found Tom Ingalls through a neighbor, and it was a natural fit. We began with the brand identity. Once we had a name, it took us a while to decide whether to be a branded house, or a house of brands.

We looked at both options seriously, and decided to be a branded house because as a craft distiller we didn't have the funds to market six different brands. We needed to put everything into one brand, and use that across our product line. That helped us make the most of our story, which is based on three things: 1) family ownership; 2) the story behind our gin and the fact that Ashby is a female distiller; and 3) grain to glass—we do everything on site. We're honest and transparent.

“ Eighty percent of our focus was on branding and marketing, because eighty percent of what sells product is your brand. Invest in a professional design firm—spend your money there. **”**

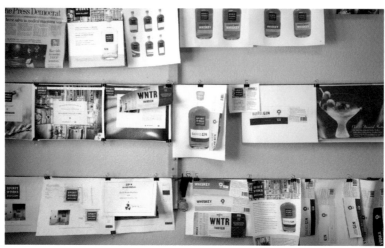

Walk us through the branding and package design process. How did you get from the initial briefing to the finished design?

We went to our first meeting at Tom's office expecting a capabilities presentation, and Tom treated the meeting as a project kick off. We talked about the ideas we had for the brand. Initially our vision was industrial and steam punk. We evolved away from steam punk eventually, and focused on industrial.

Tom put together some first round concepts. Ashby and I put together a focus group to give us input during the process. For every new phase of development, we posted the designs online for the focus group to give us feedback. It took six months to settle on becoming a branded house versus a house of brands. Then we hired a marketing person, and she helped shape the final brand logo. She pushed us to make it bolder, to have more punch, and to add the cog which became a key graphic element.

Once we had the logo, we spent about six months more on the packaging design development—the custom bottle and the label. We rejected short, fat bottles. Ashby felt the bottles weren't good in the hand—women wouldn't feel comfortable handling them.

How did you find the packaging suppliers you work with—closures, labels, glass, etc.?

Our design team recommended the screen printer. They also helped us develop the custom bottle design with the glass supplier, whom we found at an American Distilling Institute conference. The custom bottle required a large initial order, but we went for it. We liked that it was unique and our own.

What has the feedback from retailers and on-premise accounts been?

Everyone has loved and welcomed the design. It's very simple, clean and clear. It says exactly who and what it is on the front. This helps it stand out.

How did you find a distributor?

We have different distributors in every state we're in. When we decide to sell in a new market we go to the on-premise and retail accounts we want to be in, and ask who their favorite distributors are. We seek them out and make a strong presentation to them. A distributor only puts in as much effort to marketing your brand as they see you putting in yourselves.

What was the biggest challenge you encountered and how did you overcome that challenge?

We did make a change to the package early on. There was a logo on the side of the bottle, and this caused retailers to place it on the shelf sideways. So, we added the product type to the side to make it clear from that orientation too.

We encountered more challenges than we expected with the bureaucratic process of getting a distillery up and running. And, we learned that distributors won't do anything for you if you don't do anything for them—they'll deliver your product, but you have to help sell it in.

What advice do you have for distillers starting out?

It seemed to us like everyone in the industry felt like there was a race to get to market. We felt like we needed to take the time to get it all right—the product, the distillery, branding and packaging development. We spent a lot of time focusing on crossing all the t's and dotting all the i's. We're glad we did.

Eighty percent of our focus was on branding and marketing, because eighty percent of what sells product is your brand. Invest in a professional design firm—spend your money there. We feel the investment was well worth it. We have gained momentum from having a foundation that has been so well received. We knew we could get the product right, and that's critical, but the branding and marketing need a lot of time and effort.

Another big challenge was funding. Luckily we found some investors who were great financial advisors and recognized that dollars were needed for branding and marketing. For instance, our first hire was our marketing person. They also drove us to build a bigger facility and operation than we had originally envisioned because it made economic sense.

Lastly, remember to celebrate the small successes as you go, to enjoy the journey. Surround yourself with a great team—you'll be spending a lot of time together.

H. Joseph Ehrmann is the proprietor of Elixir in San Francisco. Ranked "One of the 25 Best Cocktail Bars in America" by GQ Magazine, *Elixir is known for mixing unique, hand-made cocktails and offering an extensive selection of craft spirits in an historic Old West saloon. H. Joseph was named Bartender of the Year by* Nightclub & Bar Magazine *in 2010.*

If you could name one key element that makes the most impact on-premise, would it be brand name, back-story, packaging design or another aspect of branding?
Packaging design and the brand name make the most impact. Sometimes it's the label that makes the package stand out, and sometimes it's the bottle. And, sometimes there's a great bottle, but customers can't read the name because there's not enough contrast with the label background. Brand owners should put their package in with a wall of competitors to make sure it stands out before they finalize their design.

How do you shelve and display small producers as opposed to larger national brands?
We have our spirits organized by category. We put a new brand wherever it fits on the shelf within its category. If it sells well, it moves up to the front. Unless there's a promotion and the product is getting used in a menu item, it usually doesn't get put at the front of the shelf.

What works well on the back bar?
Interesting bottle shapes are eye catching, but that's a tricky area. Bars want tall slender bottles that don't use much square footage and that work well in the hand. If a thin, broad bottle comes in, it goes in sideways. The Eighty Six Co. brand has a bottle that was designed by bartenders. This is a good example of what works in a bar.

" Brand owners should put their package in with a wall of competitors to make sure it stands out before they finalize their design.**"**

What are some things you've seen in packaging that cause problems for you?

We've had bottles come in with a neck that is either too big or too small to take a standard pour spout without spilling. We can't have leakage—it creates a mess, a loss, and a dangerous, slippery environment. Any bottle that wholesales for $35 or less gets a pour spout, and if you want to get poured frequently, make sure your bottle takes a pour spout.

We've also had some bottles that are too weak at the neck, and they snap off in a fast-paced pouring situation. The structural integrity of the glass is really important.

Closures can be a problem too—don't make it too hard for a bartender to open. We've had screw caps that spin and don't engage right, overly heavy wax dips, and corks that are too tight. These kinds of things are a barrier to success in an on-premise setting.

What questions do your customers ask when looking for a small-batch distilled spirit?

When they're looking to discover something, they start by asking what is new in a particular category, such as American whiskey, vodka, etc. They want to know what it's made from and where it's made. They ask the bartender what they think of it. If the bartender has time to talk about it, and depending on how much engagement the brand has had with my team, he or she may tell the customer the brand story.

above: H. Joseph Ehrmann at Elixir in San Francisco – photo by Darren Edwards – www.darrenedwards.com

Jason Schneider is the store manager and spirits buyer at Bottle Barn, an independently owned warehouse-style beverage retailer in Santa Rosa, California. A fan and strong supporter of craft distillers, Jason also coordinates off-site tastings and spirits education for customers and staff.

What element do you believe makes the biggest impact—brand name, back-story, packaging design or another aspect of branding?
The packaging design has the biggest impact on consumers, especially if they are not already familiar with a brand.

How do you shelve and display small producers as opposed to large national brands?
Smaller producers are stealing shelf space from the big names. Big brands that used to have multiple facings on shelf now have just one, or may be placed on end-cap displays. Significantly more of our shelf space is now dedicated to craft spirits.

What works well at retail?
People pay a premium for craft brands, and need to see the quality reflected in the look and feel of the package. This is not as critical for big brands, but essential for unknown or high-priced craft brands. Our customers look for attention to detail in design and materials—they want the label paper to feel great, and all the elements to feel hand crafted and high end.

What are some things you've seen in packaging that cause problems at retail?
Bottles that are too tall or too top heavy don't work well. Very tall bottles must be placed on the top shelf, and since that space is so limited we're less likely to take a brand on if it's too tall. Fat bottles that take up more than one slot on shelf also cause problems with shelf space, and may not be accepted. And, flimsy cases that don't stack well for display are a problem.

What questions do your customers ask when looking for a small-batch distilled spirit?
They are curious about ingredients, whether the product is organic and where is it distilled. They're looking to understand what is in the liquid, and whether it's authentically small-batch distilled.

Do customers ever ask about a brand they can describe but don't know the name of?
Yes! If they give me enough information I can probably figure out what they're looking for since I am pretty familiar with craft producers. They'll sometimes tell me they tried something at a restaurant or bar, and if they give me a few more clues, and I've been to that venue, I can often help.

As the category becomes more crowded, have you seen any brand confusion among consumers?
Not yet.

Do your customers respond best to packaging design that is more traditional in style, or more unique for its category? Do you notice a difference in what appeals to different age groups among your customers?
The retro look that's so popular right now seems to play well. Younger consumers, aged 21–35 are more drawn to craft in general. A hand-made, detailed look attracts them.

Do customers indicate that they've selected a purchase based solely on the package? If so, what did they say captured their interest about it?
Definitely. They are attracted to beautiful labels. They figure, "If they took this much effort with the packaging, the product must be great."

Tell us about some other concerns retailers have regarding package design.
We already talked about shapes and sizes. Additionally, provocative or gimmicky names and concepts that don't appeal to large groups of consumers become novelty items with a narrow audience and smaller sales volumes. We want unique and interesting offerings, but if it appeals to too few people, we know it won't sell well.

What else should producers know about branding and packaging?
Price is still a big driver in deciding what we'll carry. In order to get trial by consumers, we have to price fairly. Although we know small-batch producers have high costs, some price flexibility helps us find the right balance at retail.

How do you find the brands you carry?
Some of the brands we carry are introduced to us by distributors, and others I find through direct outreach by the distiller. Our main distributors recognized the potential in craft spirits early on, and jumped right in. We find a lot of great brands through them.

Scott Evans is Vice President of Marketing at The Henry Wine Group, a leading California distributor of wine and spirits. Scott focuses on bringing unique, authentic products to both on- and off-premise market channels.

What are retailers interested in these days—do they ask for specific product categories? Are they looking for exclusives on certain brands?

Whiskies and Bourbons are hot right now, and still have room for growth. It's hard to predict trends, but the most important thing is to have something authentic, special and unique. Be careful of building your business on something others can easily make—bitters were all the rage for a while, until the mixologists started making their own.

Retailers are interested in having brands do a special bottling just for them, as an exclusive. For instance, a whiskey producer creates a different product style, such as a single malt scotch finished in a certain way, just for one retailer so that they can offer their customers something available only at their stores.

How many craft distilled brands do you carry?

We have roughly 250 SKUs across 50 brands.

You must receive many inquiries from brand owners seeking distribution. What products interest you?

Yes, we get many inquiries, and we have to be selective. We look for things we can stand behind, that are made in small batches—grain to glass. We also consider how a brand fits with the rest of our portfolio—we avoid redundancy. We don't want too much competition between the brands within our portfolio.

What are your criteria for choosing what brands you'll distribute?

We look for great people and great stories behind the brand. Integrity is important. The people should be passionate about what they do, and do the distilling themselves. Their story should be unique and interesting. For example, we have a Bacanora in our portfolio. Bacanora is an agave distillate, made traditionally for centuries before tequila. It was outlawed during the Mexican revolution, and ours is the first legal, premium Bacanora imported into the U.S. The owner/distiller is the grandson of a distiller who made Bacanora during the revolution and they brought it back. This gives us a great story to share with retailers, and for them to share with their customers. Its uniqueness grabs people's attention.

What are some craft distilled spirits brands that do well for you? What it is about these brands that makes them successful?

We have a Cachaça, which is a traditional Brazilian spirit, and we kicked off marketing it with the World Cup. The daughter of our Pisco producer lives in San Francisco and helps us with marketing their brand, Capurro. What does well for us are brands with regionality and a grass-roots feel, supported by a strong story and family ownership—people want to feel like they're a part of something interesting. They want to be able to tell their friends.

Do you carry brands from other states/regions, or only your local region?

We carry many imports, and things from across the United States, like Boyd and Blair Vodka from Pennsylvania. They have a great following. It's important to build a following in your own region, and then move into other regions with that track record.

What are some key points of differentiation that make one distiller stand out vs. competitors?

If you have a unique process—say an amaro that was finished with a different technique—make that known, but also make it understandable for the consumer. Don't get overly complicated in your explanation. It's good to be edgy and cool, but not off-putting. Be consistent and concise, but with a little bit of mystery. Your story can do this, and your packaging can do it too—have a cool edge while also connecting with the audience.

❝ Unique is good, but you can be too unique. A package should fit its category. I see traditional packages giving good results. The best are traditional with a fresh, unique feel.❞

Small batch producers often lack the capital and know-how to efficiently market their product. What do producers need to focus on so that their distributor has something to leverage in marketing a brand?

Regionality—start by being relevant in your own region and grow as the market allows you to grow. If you're in Sonoma, California, and sell your product in Petaluma, California, make sure you have a strong base of loyal customers to test your product, package and story. Make sure you have something compelling before moving into new markets.

Also make sure that story is relevant to your product—it's not just about you. Your story needs to link to how and why you make what you make. And don't get jaded about your own story—don't stop telling it because you're tired of hearing it.

Would you say retailers respond best to packaging design that is fairly traditional, or unique for the category? Do you notice a difference in what appeals to different types of retailers or different regions?

Unique is good, but you can be too unique. A package should fit its category. I see traditional packages giving good results. The best are traditional with a fresh, unique feel. Again, regionality is something I think should be reflected in your package. A New York product should look different from an Oregon product—the font style should reference that region. Your label should also help tell your story. Next, your bottle shape should fit your category. Stay within your realm, but be interesting.

Consistency is important—in packaging, pricing, production. Define your pricing model before you go into the market. Don't misjudge that and then take a price increase after you've gotten a following.

Lastly, invest in your packaging. I've seen some distillers who do everything well, but then don't invest in their packaging. Think it through—don't be too gimmicky or cheap.

above:

DISTILLERY   2 BAR SPIRITS

PACKAGE DESIGN   Jay Mollet

opposite page:

DISTILLERY   HUMBOLDT DISTILLERY

PACKAGE DESIGN   Auston Design Group

below:

DISTILLERY   LYON DISTILLING CO.

PACKAGE DESIGN   FUNNEL : Eric Kass

opposite page:

DISTILLERY   3 HOWLS DISTILLERY

PACKAGE DESIGN   Force & Form

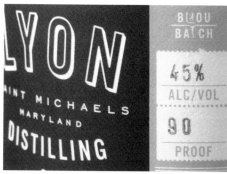

DISTILLERY   CARDINAL SPIRITS

PACKAGE DESIGN   Adam Quirk & Ryan Irvin

DISTILLERY   VENUS SPIRITS
PACKAGE DESIGN   Chen Design Associates

|29|

HUDSON
BABY BOURBON
WHISKEY

375 ml   46% alc/vol
Made with 100% New York Corn
Aged under 4 yrs in American Oak
Handmade and Bottled by:
Tuthilltown Spirits, Gardiner, New York

375 ml   46% alc/vol
Made with 100% Malted Barl
Aged Under 4 Years in Oak
Hand Crafted and Bottled by
town Spirits, Gardiner, New

HUDSON
FOUR GRAIN BOURBON
WHISKEY

375 ml   46% alc/vol
Pot-Distilled From Corn, Rye, Wheat & Barley
Aged Under Four Years In Oak
Hand Crafted And Bottled By:
Tuthilltown Spirits, Gardiner, New York

HATTAN RYE
HISKEY

375 ml   46% alc/vol
Distilled From Rye Grain
New Oak Less Than Four Years
and Crafted and Bottled by:
town Spirits, Gardiner, New York.

DISTILLERY   TUTHILLTOWN SPIRITS
PACKAGE DESIGN   Ralph Erenzo

DISTILLERY   OLD HARBOR DISTILLING CO.

PACKAGE DESIGN   Caava Design

DISTILLERY   FEW SPIRITS

PACKAGE DESIGN   Wilburn Thomas

GLASS
OPTIONS FOR A CRITICAL COMPONENT
BY ERICA HILLER HARROP OF GLOBAL PACKAGE LLC.

Erica Hiller Harrop is the owner of Global Package, LLC. Global Package specializes in glass and closures for wine and spirits. Erica has been working with glass producers internationally since the mid 1980s.

STOCK VS. CUSTOM BOTTLES

The bottle you choose for your package has a big impact on the first impression and overall quality communication made by your brand. It sets the expectations for your product style and quality. A heavy bottle with quality elements such as a crest or embossing will communicate that care and effort was put into making the product, just as effort was put into the fine characteristics of the bottle.

Although the cost of a high-quality bottle may feel like a stretch for a startup budget, using the right glass from the beginning is important. Modifying the label size and ordering different materials later will cost more in the long run. And, not having the right bottle will undermine your brand's image during the critical "first impression" stage of launch.

STOCK BOTTLES

There are many stock bottle options available. European glass suppliers offer very creative options and they are continually developing new bottles and carafes. It is not difficult to find stock bottles for quantities as low as 100 cases worth. European bottles come in bulk on pallets, so shipping cartons and gift boxes must be purchased separately.

SEMI-CUSTOM

Glass specialists travel to China to create and import their own designs at affordable prices for semi-custom shapes. Chinese bottle quality varies, and it's important to work with a proven supplier to ensure American standards are met. Because production costs are lower in China there are more opportunities to modify bottle elements and obtain a unique design.

CUSTOM

A custom bottle shape designed and produced specifically for your brand conveys the highest quality message because it communicates a larger investment in the brand. There are some limitations to creating a custom bottle beside the one-time investment in the development of the bottle molds: the minimum run size is at least 1,000 cases and may be as high as 3,000 cases.

The cost of most custom bottles will be 40% higher for smaller production runs, but, at quantities above 5,000 cases pricing begins to be within 20% of the cost of a semi-standard bottle at the same weight.

Besides quantity and price, the weight of the glass is a factor. Standard bottles weight 500 grams (1.1 lbs), whereas thick-based bottles weigh around 800 grams (1.8 lbs). Not all factories will make these heavier weight bottles or do it well. The shape of the bottle will also affect the price. Square and unusual shapes are more difficult to make and the price will reflect this.

SUSTAINABILITY OF GLASS: RECYCLED BOTTLES

All bottles are made from recycled glass because it lowers the amount of raw material needed and reduces the amount of energy required to melt the raw materials: soda ash, sand and limestone. Recycled content can range from 25% to 95%, but most fall in the range of 40% recycled content. Because glass does not degrade with multiple recycling, it's a highly sustainable material.

WEIGHT AND THE CARBON FOOTPRINT

Bottles have become lighter in weight over the past 30 years as the quality of forming equipment and inspection machines has improved. Bottles weighing 420 grams (0.925 lbs) can now easily be manufactured, whereas the heaviest ones weigh 1.2 kg (2.64 lbs). Although less environmentally friendly, heavy bottles are popular because the luxury market wants the variety and cult appeal.

However, concerns about wastefulness are valid and many specialty shapes are being made at lighter weights, allowing a craft look with a lower carbon footprint. The benefits of lighter bottles are not only lower production costs and lower emission of noxious gasses during melting, but also the final product will weigh less and take up less room during transportation.

Each brand owner must balance the cost and sustainability differences between lighter and heavier bottles against the luxury appeal of heavier glass and make an informed decision that fits their branding and sustainability goals.

QUALITY PERCEPTION BEGINS WITH FIRST IMPRESSIONS

Glass bottles are the perfect vessel for keeping a liquid safe and unaffected by oxygen, and do not extract flavors or allow any leaching of outside elements. But mostly, a bottle can be beautifully shaped—which is key to a successful and lasting impression. It sets the tone for your brand personality, conveys the quality of your product, and becomes a key part of brand recognition, allowing consumers to spot and recognize your brand on a shelf or back bar quickly.

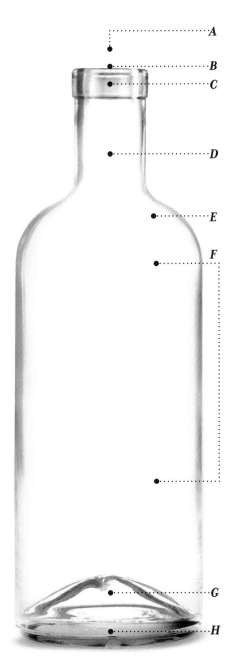

A. ***Through Bore*** — This refers to the minimum neck diameter for ease in bottling. A fill tube must typically be at least 1 mm narrower than the through bore. For example, if a through bore is 16.5 mm, then the fill tube is recommended to be 15.5 mm. Normal filling tubes are 15 mm or larger.

B. ***Bore*** — This term refers to the dimension at the very top opening of the bottle and tells the bottler what size cork should be used for the best seal. Standard bore for the U.S. is 18.5 mm (0.728 inch). Many larger-necked spirits bottles use 21.5 mm (0.846 inch) or larger. The length of the bore inside of the neck is important for ensuring proper cork sealing.

C. ***Bottle Ring*** — Sometimes called the bead, this is the flared top section of the bottle. A seam on the lower edge of the ring shows where this part of the mold is joined to the body mold. The bottle ring can be interchanged with a compatible body mold.

D. ***Bottle Neck*** — This part of the bottle takes on a difficult task when air is blown into the bottle. It must be straight inside and out, creating a controlled cylinder for the cork to fit in. A thin neck takes a smaller diameter cork, while a fat neck will require a larger cork.

E. ***Shoulder*** — The widest part at the top of the body, just below the neck. If embossing is used, it is usually applied here because this area has no bottle-to-bottle contact point when bottles stand side-by-side.

F. ***Label Panel*** — The bottle blueprint shows the location and size of the label panel. Designers should use this reference to ensure the label fits on this flat area.

G. ***Punt*** — This pushed-up area is a traditional addition to the bottle. It has no real use in current glassmaking, but some consider a deep punt to be an indication of quality. The punt can add height to a bottle by taking up volume in the base, and can be customized.

H. ***Base*** — The bottom of the bottle has a base plate where the base attaches to the body mold. This area can be customized.

above:

DISTILLERY DOUBLE V DISTILLERY

PACKAGE DESIGN Sasquatch Agency

opposite page:

DISTILLERY HOUSE SPIRITS DISTILLERY

PACKAGE DESIGN Sandstrom Partners

above:

DISTILLERY .... VENUS SPIRITS

PACKAGE DESIGN .... Chen Design Associates

opposite page:

DISTILLERY .... KOVAL

PACKAGE DESIGN .... Dando Projects

WOODINVILLE WHISKEY CO.

ONE HUNDRED PERCENT RYE WHISKEY

HANDCRAFTED

BATCH NO. 13

BOTTLE NO. 3331

Crafted entirely by hand in small batches from 100% rye and aged to maturity in new, charred, oak barrels. This demanding process results in an extremely rich and full-bodied rye whiskey.

MICROBARRELED

46% ALC/VOL • 750 ML • Made in Washington

DISTILLERY   WOODINVILLE WHISKEY CO.

PACKAGE DESIGN   David Cole Creative

DISTILLERY .... KINGS COUNTY DISTILLERY ....
PACKAGE DESIGN ...... In-house ....

KINGS COUNTY DISTILLERY
moonshine
corn whiskey 200ml
40% alcohol by volume

KINGS COUNTY DISTILLERY
bourbon whiskey
45% alcohol by volume, 200ml

DISTILLERY .... OLE SMOKY DISTILLERY

PACKAGE DESIGN .... In-house

DISTILLERY   FÅR NORTH SPIRITS

PACKAGE DESIGN   Jenney Stevens

DISTILLERY No. 209

FOUNDER Leslie Rudd   **EST.** 2005

SPIRITS   GIN & VODKA

LOCATION   San Francisco, California

PACKAGE DESIGN Through Smoke,
Jim Cross and Madeleine Corson

San Francisco's Distillery No. 209 was founded by Leslie Rudd, an entrepreneur whose passion for best-in-class wine and food has driven him to build several businesses. After he purchased the historic Edge Hill property in Napa Valley, he noticed the faintly visible words "Registered Distillery No. 209" painted above the iron doors of what was being used as a hay barn. We spoke with Wendi Green, a member of the Distillery No. 209 team, to unearth the rest of the story.

What inspired you to start a distillery?

Distillery No. 209 traces its origins to 1882 when vintner-distiller William Scheffler added a stone and brick distillery to the winemaking facilities at Edge Hill Estate in St. Helena, California. A distiller at heart, Scheffler registered the distillery with the federal government and was given distillery license number 209 — the 209th distillery permitted by law in the U.S. Scheffler's distilled spirits were very high quality, winning a medal at the Universal Exposition of 1889 in Paris, France.

In 1999, Leslie Rudd became the new steward of the Edge Hill Estate. He decided to revive the distilling operation after learning the rich history, and re-established the distillery at Pier 50 in San Francisco, adjacent to AT&T Park.

above: the original Distillery No. 209
right: Master Distiller Arne Hillesland

Who designed your brand identity and packaging?

The original inspiration for the No. 209 Gin bottle came from an old Genevers bottle that Leslie Rudd, our founder, discovered at a gin museum in Holland. The way in which the wide shoulders taper down was originally due to manufacturing limitations of the time. Having the bottom of the bottle more narrow than the top allowed for the bottles to be removed from the glass molds more easily.

We took the original Genever bottle and contracted a glass manufacturer to create a prototype of the bottle that integrated modifications that we wanted to make. A punt was put in our bottle as homage to our winemaking roots in Napa Valley. There is also a small symbol in the punt that was once the symbol of a Dutch glass making guild that means "perfection in glass." The crest on the back of the bottle is the family crest of General Keyes, one of the original owners of Edge Hill Winery in St. Helena (Napa Valley).

No single person is responsible for the branding and packaging design of our bottle. Many designers were responsible for parts of the design to get our bottle where it is today. Designers that were involved in the process include Through Smoke, Jim Cross and Madeleine Corson.

Many iterations of the bottle were done in addition to different decoration including various colors and applications, and a paper label at one point that never made it to final production. The typography used today is a replica of the original fonts found on the historic distillery in St. Helena.

> **" A piece of advice I wish I had been given when I started out: marketing is the hardest and most important thing. "**
>
> —Leslie Rudd

Tell us about the journey from the idea of launching a spirits brand to the actual launch. How long did it take to get product ready for sale?

The initial journey began in 1999 when Leslie Rudd purchased the historic Edge Hill Estate and discovered the original distillery building on the property. Research was done for a few years until he committed to restarting the distillery in 2003, eventually launching to market in 2005.

While working on the bottle design, the distillery was being constructed in San Francisco and the recipe was formulated and tweaked over this period as well. A more citrus-forward, modern style gin recipe was crafted and is still the same recipe used today.

How did you find the packaging suppliers you work with for closures, labels, glass, etc.?

We currently work with Waterdogs. There are many glass manufacturers including Saverglass, Bruni, etc, so once you have a concept, you just need to reach out to any number of companies to start the design process or work directly with a broker. Our entire bottle, including capsule and packaging, comes from the same factory to ensure quality and consistency.

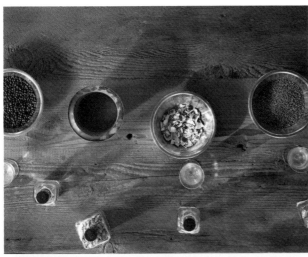

What has the feedback from retailers and on-premise accounts been?

We've always received compliments on our packaging in terms of it being elegant and classic, yet edgy. The historical elements that were integrated into the package help tell the history of the distillery and owners to create an extremely unique package.

How did you find a distributor?

Our founder started his career in the distribution business, so he called on his many contacts over the years. He also hired John Olson, a long-time industry veteran to launch the brand in multiple markets.

What was the biggest challenge you encountered? How did you overcome that challenge?

The biggest challenge is to get attention in the crowded marketplace, especially considering that much of the competition comes from large conglomerates that have leverage across brands. At the outset, it's difficult to get a distributor to take a chance on a small brand that doesn't have the same marketing and advertising pockets of the large suppliers.

If there is one piece of advice you wish someone had told you starting out, what would it be?

"Marketing is the hardest and most important thing." — Leslie Rudd

Your package plays a central role in initiating a consumer's first purchase. Said another way, the first sale is the label, the second is the product inside. Your label attracts the eye, pulls in the consumer's attention and then captures their imagination. Whether to use a direct screen-printed bottle or a paper label is an important branding and marketing decision. It is not uncommon in the craft spirits world to see a combination of the two, which is visually appealing, although more expensive.

ADVANTAGES OF SCREEN-PRINTING VS. PAPER LABELS

Screen-printing offers practical advantages over paper labels, since it eliminates the cost of label application and is more durable. First, screen-printed, decorated bottles arrive at the distillery ready to be filled, eliminating the cost and time required to operate a labeling machine or hand-apply labels. As your business scales up and your output increases, hand label application will require an unsustainable amount of labor. Don't be surprised if the cost of hand application is greater than the cost of screen-printing. A second practical advantage is the extreme durability of a ceramic screen-printed label. A ceramic label won't tear, rip or wrinkle during shipping and handling, and it won't be damaged by spills in an on-premise environment. This reduces waste and ensures that your brand always looks its best.

The brand owner who chooses screen-printing is seeking a unique look. While screen-printing is often associated with high-end packages, it can be used to create a higher perceived value for products at any price point. It reinforces the prestige of the brand and supports the retail price. Specialty inks such as precious gold and silver can also be used to underscore the quality of the product. These metallic inks deliver the richness and sparkle of true gold or silver, and the luxury perception that comes with it.

EXPANDED DESIGN OPTIONS

Screen printing offers exciting design possibilities and the technique can be applied across all design styles, ranging from the classic and sophisticated to bold and fun. From a branding perspective, screen-printing enables your entire bottle to serve as a canvas of visual expression. A full wrap label, be it on a round or square bottle, can maximize the graphic impact of your design. The consumer will hold that bottle in their hand for just a little bit longer than normal as they turn the bottle around to view the entire label.

And, depending on the decorator that you work with, you may be able to explore neck and shoulder printing. Neck printing has long been used by the beer industry. It can easily be applied to the spirits industry and offers another way to catch consumers' attention. Shoulder printing is more technical and requires the perfect 'marriage' between the artwork and the bottle. An experienced decorator will determine how the art file should be prepared to facilitate the wrapping of the print up the bottle shoulder.

opposite page:

DISTILLERY   HELLO CELLO

PACKAGE DESIGN   Alternatives NY

SCREEN-PRINTED BY MONVERA GLASS DÉCOR

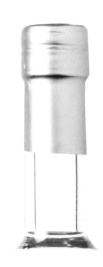

BUILD A COLLABORATIVE TEAM

Regardless of the type of label that you envision for your product, it is important to assemble a packaging team early to make sure the design is optimized for your print process. This team should consist of a professional and experienced label designer, the bottle supplier and the decorator.

Everyone will need to work together to make sure the label being designed can be applied to the desired bottle and can be printed within a predetermined budget. Too often, labels are designed that can't be produced on the already purchased glass or can't be produced by the decorator within a certain cost framework. Before you dive too far into the design process, make sure that your team understands your budget, your time-frame and the bottle choices that you are considering. Collaboration in the early stages can prevent disappointment along with lost time and resources later.

Screen-printing is now a viable label consideration for most craft spirits. Costs have come down in recent years due to new manufacturing capacity. The biggest factor that impacts price is volume. Screen-printing is cost competitive against paper labels at lower volumes, especially for small lot runs. At higher volumes, screen-printing costs more than a paper label, but a more streamlined bottling process offsets some of this cost.

Don't make the mistake of not allocating enough budget for the package and going to market with a label that is inferior to the quality of the product. Instead of hoping that you'll sell enough to upgrade the package in the future, launch with a strong package that what will set the tone for your brand.

this page:
DISTILLERY   TUTHILLTOWN SPIRITS
PACKAGE DESIGN   Fahrenheit 212, NY

far left:
DISTILLERY   RICHLAND DISTILLING
PACKAGE DESIGN   Erik Vonk and Karin Vonk
(owners)/Beth Cendere Design LLC.

left:
DISTILLERY   FLAGHILL SPIRITS
PACKAGE DESIGN   In-house

DISTILLERY   10th MOUNTAIN WHISKEY & SPIRIT CO.

PACKAGE DESIGN   970 Design

DRINK TO GLORY

10TH MOUNTAIN
WHISKEY & SPIRIT
COMPANY
VAIL COLORADO

10

AGED
IN NEW OAK
BARRELS FOR
6
MONTHS

750ML

MOUNTAIN STRO

DISTILLER: KAYLA
BATCH#: 1
BOTTLED: 9·10·14

DISTILLERY ···· *7 STILLS OF SAN FRANCISCO*
PACKAGE DESIGN ···· *7 Stills & Zio Ziegler*

DISTILLERY .... OOLA DISTILLERY
PACKAGE DESIGN .... Piper Design Co.

DISTILLERY   ROGUE SPIRITS
PACKAGE DESIGN   In-house

DISTILLERY   PEACH STREET DISTILLERS
PACKAGE DESIGN   RTO+P

DISTILLERY   KOVAL
PACKAGE DESIGN   Dando Projects

FALCON SPIRITS, LLC

CASE STUDY

FOUNDER Farid Dormishian   EST. 2013

SPIRITS   GIN, LIQUEURS, RUM, AMAROS

LOCATION   Richmond, California

PACKAGE DESIGN   Botanica Spiritus: Ignite

Falcon Spirits Liqueur: Cult Partners

A former biochemist, Farid Dormishian of Falcon Spirits dabbled in home winemaking and distillation for years before deciding to blend his passion for spirits, science and business to pursue distilling full time. Falcon currently makes a western style gin, and will soon release a new dry style gin and a barrel-aged gin. Seasonal liqueurs, including a dry Raspberry liqueur, are another focus. And he's developing amaros, whiskey, and rum.

What inspired you to start a distillery?

My grandmother was a great cook and made infused liqueurs on her farm. I spent summers there, and learned to respect the land and the labor that goes into what we have on our table. I went on to study Biochemistry at U.C. Berkeley, where I conducted my undergraduate research project on fermentation. To pay for tuition, I worked as a bartender—I was a mixologist 20 years ago, researching old recipes, and creating new ones using fresh ingredients, infusions, and homemade bitters. I worked for 20 years in biotech, and found it rewarding. Meanwhile, I made wine for family consumption, dabbled in distillation, and developed an interest in some of the handcrafted spirits being made. I was interested in herbs and distilling them using water vapor.

I took a detour to study business, getting MBAs in management and finance. Finance intrigued me. I ended up working for a great university, but I didn't enjoy my particular role as much as I'd thought.

How did you come up with your brand name and what is the meaning behind it?

Falcon and Botanica Spiritus were not my first choices—so many names were already taken. That's one thing that's important in starting this kind of business—you need to be able to shift gears or change focus. I settled on Botanica because the spirit of the plant is what I'm trying to capture in the bottle. The ancient Greeks believed aroma was the spirit of the plant.

I chose the name Falcon Spirits because falcons are very graceful, fast and beautiful. This fits with my high standards.

Farid Dormishian of Falcon Spirits Distillery

Tell us about your journey from the idea of launching a spirits brand to the actual launch.

The idea first occurred to me when I was bartending. I heard about Germain-Robin and St. George, but was too entrenched in biotech. Helping people by curing diseases seemed more important. About three years ago I took a year off to research distillation. I traveled to places where I could learn about distilling, herbs, perfume making—I took classes and did internships in the U.S. and Europe. I also did a lot of experimentation on my own.

With my business education, I was able to create a business plan. I had to do that from scratch, because there wasn't much information available about what was required to start a micro-distillery.

It took me six months to find my location. I settled on Richmond, California, because it has great water for my process, and I am next to the bay. It took a year and a half to build the distillery and pass all the regulations—there were many unexpected delays with permits and TTB approval. Along the way, I lost my father, who was also my biggest supporter.

Once you had a brand name, how did you find a designer to help with branding and packaging design?

I looked at a lot of design online and found Ignite in Portland. I worked with them on Botanica Spiritus Gin. Their style was in line with my vision for the gin. I had a concern about working long distance, but it was not a problem. I went up to Portland to meet the owner Mr. Dave Bourne, but probably didn't need to do so.

Then I worked with Cult Partners for the Falcon Spirits liqueur because I wanted something more modern—we use a modern process for our liqueurs. I found Cult Partners the same way—I saw some of their work and reached out to them.

> **"** Word of mouth doesn't get you far — you need to be out in the field selling, and you need tools for marketing your brand. **"**

Walk us through the branding and package design process. How did you get from the initial briefing to the finished design?

I had an idea for the look I wanted for the gin. I gathered images that interested me—lettering styles, wax finishes, corks, designs—and kept a scrapbook. Dave, from Ignite, then filtered them into six different designs that all fit. It was difficult to choose between them, but I was able to settle on one.

How did you find the packaging suppliers you work with—closures, labels, glass, etc?

I did online searches and called people in the industry. Dave provided some resources as well. We had to switch label printers and bottle suppliers due to some problems. Our first run of labels came back looking nothing like I'd expected, and the printer wasn't very accommodating about fixing it. That cost us some money. And, our bottle supplier changed from a European manufacturer to a Chinese one without telling us. The bottles came back smelling like fish, and I had to warehouse them away from the distillery and spend extra money cleaning them.

I've changed both my label printer and bottle company to suppliers that understand how important quality is to us. Quality is essential, even if it costs a bit more. And, I learned that you must do a press check when you run your labels to make sure the finished labels match your vision. The first time I was busy and didn't go—I didn't know how critical that was.

What has the feedback from retailers and on-premise accounts been?

I make a very aromatic gin and a lot of people like it. But, educating bartenders about how to use it in drinks has been a marketing focus for us. It's great served neat, is great in a Bees Knees and it works well with bitter flavors. However, not all tonics work with it. Based on a suggestion from our marketing person, we put a drinks page up on our website.

How did you find a distributor?

This was a hard decision—I debated whether I should go with a big distributor or a small one. I think small distributors are better for a small brand because the brand gets lost with a big distributor. Our small distributor takes the time to educate people about our products. The bigger guys might get you more placements, but won't get you as much support. There's a limit to how much I can produce currently, so the quality of placement is very important to building my brand and its reputation.

What was the biggest challenge you encountered?

The Botanica name on our label is much bigger than Spiritus. This has caused confusion in bars because another brand has a similar sounding name to Botanica. Bartenders automatically grab the similarly named bigger brand, and we lose sales. It's important to have a very clear and distinctive name when you're small so that people recognize it right away.

Sales is our biggest challenge on an ongoing basis. It requires a lot of time and personal attention from me. Word of mouth doesn't get you far—you need to be out in the field selling, and you need tools for marketing your brand.

What advice do you wish someone had told you starting out?

Being well funded is really important. The risk of failure is very high if you are not well capitalized. Don't give up your day job until you're sure you're profitable. Even with my finance background I underestimated the costs involved in my start up. The growth rate is very slow. All of our revenue goes back into the business.

It's not all about distilling. There's lots of other stuff—from fixing the boiler to all the business management. Without funds to hire help, you have to do everything yourself. This cuts into sales time and slows your growth. Be prepared to sleep at the distillery because you don't have time to go home. You must be ready to do whatever it takes twelve hours a day, seven days a week, for several years.

PAPER LABELS
PROCESS AND POSSIBILITIES

David Busé is President of Collotype Labels in Napa, California. Collotype is one of the leading print-ers for premium wine and spirits, with locations around the world. They produce labels for regional boutique brands and multi-million-case global brands alike. We talked with David about label printing considerations in general, focusing on the specific concerns of small batch distillers.

PRINTING IS AN ART AS WELL AS A SCIENCE

A beautifully printed paper label helps your package communicate quality and supports a premium price point. A common mistake among brand owners is assuming that once the artwork is done, and the proofs approved, the print process is simply about executing per the specs. In reality, there is much fine-tuning needed to translate a design concept into ink on paper.

Printing is a surprisingly variable process, and a well-printed label that arrives in market looking its best is the result of a carefully controlled, focused collaboration between the designer, brand owner and printer.

PRINTING METHODS AND COST

Like many kinds of production, setup drives most of the cost of printing. Whether your order calls for 1,000 labels or 50,000 labels, the setup and custom tooling needed is the same. Therefore, smaller quantities have a higher per-unit price because setup costs get amortized across fewer units.

Fortunately, there are more options than ever before for small producers. Digital presses offer lower cost for small print runs, but are not the right fit for every project. In some cases, traditional lithographic or flexographic printing may cost less than digital.

CONVENTIONAL PRESSES

With conventional lithographic and flexographic printing, the cost of printing plates and preparing the press for each job is significant. However, if your label has multiple embellishments, such as foil stamp-ing and embossing, conventional printing may offer greater economy because these treatments are built into the press, and can be applied in the same pass as the inks.

DIGITAL PRESSES

Digital printing helps reduce the cost of shorter runs because there are no plates to buy and you don't have to shut down the press to change information between SKUs. Digital printing is also a good choice if you have variable or sequential data on your label, such as bottle numbering. Even your image could change across the run.

On the other hand, embellishments such as foil stamping and embossing require a second pass through the press for digital labels, whereas they can be done in one pass on a flexographic or lithographic press.

Collotype usually prices each job both ways, because the variables between label designs make it hard to predict whether digital or conventional printing will give the best price, even for a short print run.

SPECIALTY TREATMENTS

Foil stamping, embossing, custom label shapes and other value-added treatments are common on spirits labels, and can increase the perceived value of your package, resulting in stronger sales. They do, however, require a higher initial investment in your packaging compared to straight ink on paper.

❝ Spirits labels are little works of art and the most important billboard for your brand. Especially for small producers, your package will be the only marketing tool working for you when you're not there.❞

—David Busé

Most labels today are printed on pressure-sensitive (or self-adhesive) paper stock. The paper comes on a roll, called a web. With pressure-sensitive labels, custom label shapes and sizes cost no more than standard rectangles since a cutting die is required for all labels.

Foil stamping requires an added investment both in the tooling and the foil itself, and it also adds setup time on press. Embossing is less costly than foil because there is no material cost—just the cost of tooling.

Another enhancement that gives paper labels a premium look is what we call a high-build varnish—a silk-screened effect that sits on the surface of the paper and creates an embossed look. This costs less than foil or embossing, although there is some cost in making the screen.

Bear in mind that tooling costs might be very high at your start up volumes, but that investment will set you up well for future growth. Those dies will be used from year to year, and over time your volume will bring your unit cost down.

COLLABORATION ENSURES THE BEST RESULT AT THE LOWEST COST

The distiller and designer should meet with the label printer to review the design and discuss cost and options available as early as possible—even at the concept stage. This allows for collaboration and op- tions- analysis to achieve the best result for the lowest cost. And, it prevents a brand owner from falling in love with an idea that can't be executed. Lastly, it gives the printer time to source unusual elements or materials if needed.

As soon as you have a preliminary design concept, have your designer prepare preliminary specifications so that you can review them with printers and select a printer that best meets your needs. The print team's expertise can be invaluable in saving time and money, along with avoiding design problems that create performance issues in label application or during the shipping of product.

KOVAL
DRY GIN
distilled from organic grains
HANDMADE IN CHICAGO
47% Alc. By Vol. 750ml

DISTILLERY   KOVAL

PACKAGE DESIGN   Dando Projects

PRELIMINARY PROOFING OPTIONS

Proofing systems that simulate the finished, printed label are helpful for previewing results. Good printers can now provide digitally printed proofs for a few hundred dollars, and multiple options can be included on one sheet. These won't include foil stamping, die cutting or embossing, but they give a very good indication of colors. Many printers also offer ink jet proofs that are calibrated to mimic the settings on their press, and these can give a good approximation of the finished label.

New ways to preview your label before committing ink to paper expand as technology improves. Collotype has a tool called the Visualizer, which is a virtual-reality based tool. A video shows the front and back of the bottle, simulating a photo of the final label.

PRESS PROOFING AND PRESS CHECKS

After preliminary proofs have been carefully checked and approved it's time to take the label on press. Reviewing and fine-tuning results on press is an essential step in ensuring the proper execution of the design.

One option is a press proof. During a press proof, the printer sets up the job on the press and runs samples for review and input, prior to the production run. This is valuable when fine-tuning color is necessary or if you want to check how different elements work together in real life. A press proofing typically costs $2,500 to $3,000.

When that's not in the budget, a press check should be planned. This means that the designer and the customer are on-site for the production run, giving them the opportunity to review the labels and make small refinements to dial everything in before the printer runs the job. This doesn't add cost, and is highly recommended for all new labels.

INK DRAWDOWNS

If your label calls for custom ink colors, you should request ink drawdowns beforehand to review and approve before the print run. Drawdowns are swatches made from the specified inks on the specified paper stock.

For Pantone colors it's best if the printer matches the actual Pantone chips. Make sure your designer uses a coated chip reference for coated paper stock and an uncoated chip reference for uncoated stock. Inks look very different on different paper surfaces because of the way the ink absorbs into the paper.

LABEL APPLICATION OPTIONS

Most small producers apply their labels by hand. There are semi-automated setups that hold the bottle in place so that the labels go on straight and in the same location every time, and while not nearly as fast as a fully automated labeler, they do speed up the process somewhat.

Although hand application is a viable option for small bottlings, a new brand should think about how their labels will be applied when they grow their volume. At large volumes, hand labeling may become too costly and too slow. Make sure an automated bottling line can apply your label when the time comes.

LABEL PAPER STOCKS

Papers are a key element in conveying the essence of your brand. Considerations include the look of gloss versus uncoated paper, sustainability factors such as recycled content, and whether a product will be in a wet environment such as the cold box or ice bucket and need a wet-strength stock.

Paper conveys a tremendous amount about product quality and even the nature of the product itself. For instance, an organic brand may want to use an FSC-certified stock, which comes with the right to use the Forest Sustainability Council logo on your label.

One factor that is rarely considered is sizing the label to maximize the width of the roll of paper. Paper cost is significant, so if your label size can fit more than once across the width of the roll, that reduces costs.

OTHER CONSIDERATIONS

Spirits labels are little works of art and the most important billboard for your brand. Especially for small producers, your package will be the only marketing tool working for you when you're not there. Label design and printing is not a place to skimp.

A well-executed label is a joint effort between the designer and the team of craftsman in the printing plant, including the ink technician, the pre-press team who prepares your files to print, and your press operator. During printing, paper follows a 200 to 300 foot path through the printing press. Many variables can create challenges along this path. Very tight registration is expected between inks and other embellishments in order to end up with a seamless, high quality finished label. With collaboration, the printing of your label can be one of the most exciting and gratifying parts of the branding process.

SONOMA COUNTY DISTILLING CO.

CASE STUDY

FOUNDER	Adam Boyd Spiegel EST. 2010*
SPIRITS	RYE, BOURBON, WHEAT WHISKEY, FUTURE FRUIT BRANDIES & GRAPPAS
LOCATION	Rohnert Park, California
PACKAGE DESIGN	Mary Lee Designs

* rebranded in 2013

Owner and distiller Adam Boyd Spiegel established Sonoma County Distilling Company in Rohnert Park, California, after buying out a previous business partner and rebranding his product line in 2013. In just two years, he has quadrupled his production and sales volume. The distillery produces four different whiskies, and is also developing fruit brandies that leverage Sonoma County's amazing fruit, such as apples from orchards in Sebastopol.

What inspired you to start a distillery?

I come from a finance background. When the economy crashed I decided it was time for a change and that I should pursue a career that allowed me to develop a skill set over the course of my life. I had dabbled in distilling, and decided that was what I wanted to do.

How did you come up with your brand name and what is the meaning behind it?

The name we started with, 1512 Spirits, came from a previous business, and wasn't especially meaningful when we split. After the buy out, I rebranded the company as Sonoma County Distilling Company because we're located at the gateway to the Sonoma region and I want to reflect the best of this area. We make our products all in-house, grain to glass, and our approach fits with Sonoma's handmade-from-scratch, "Slow Food" sensibility.

Adam Boyd Spiegel of Sonoma County Distilling

Tell us about your journey from the idea of launching a spirits brand to the actual launch.

It took a year to get up and running. The city of Rohnert Park previously had no distilleries, so we had to lay the groundwork, teaching the city about our business. In 2011 we started producing clear spirits. We have a short-term aging program in small barrels, which allows us to make a great product more quickly. Our philosophy is not to over-oak spirits, but to finesse the spirit, crafting a whiskey that is rounded, intentioned, and sophisticated.

Once you had a brand name, how did you find a designer to help with branding and packaging design?

A mutual friend of the distillery introduced us to designer Mary Lee. It's a collaborative process—we have a strong vision that drives our design, and we do a lot of design work in-house ourselves. We've built a good working relationship with Mary Lee over the life of the business.

Walk us through the branding and package design process. How did you get from the initial briefing to the finished design?

To start, we showed our designer reference of designs that were similar to the idea we had for our label. Next, we looked at lots of design options—several rounds—that Mary Lee created. After exploring creative options, we started over to get back to our very simple, uncluttered vision. We wanted only the necessary information on the label. "Handcrafted" is the key communication we wanted to come through.

❝ From a branding standpoint, my advice is: don't try to be totally different. Just try to be as "you" as you can be. You need to feel excited about it and it has to be a reflection of who you are. ❞

How did you find the packaging suppliers you work with—closures, labels, glass, etc.?

Mostly through referrals. We had to find a stock bottle that fits our type of spirit because we are operating on a shoestring. We've been through a couple of glass suppliers. We decided not to go with Chinese glass due to quality concerns, even though our Italian glass costs more.

We started out buying seals and corks in local homebrew supply shops, and eventually found a wholesale supplier in California. We use string around the neck of our bottles, and we originally purchased it retail from a local fabric store. They eventually connected us with their supplier to buy direct, in bulk.

We found our printer through an online search. They're in Colorado, which is a bit of a problem if the labels aren't correct, but it's usually okay. We really value the suppliers who go the extra mile for small producers. These relationships are really important to us.

What has the feedback from retailers and on-premise accounts been?

Jason at Bottle Barn in Santa Rosa and our local grocery store, Oliver's Market, have been great supporters from day one.

How did you find a distributor?

We've gone through several distributors, big and small, and are now working in California with Young's Market in their Craft Spirits portfolio.

What was the biggest challenge you encountered and how did you overcome that challenge?

We ran into a challenge with applying our packaging as we increased volume. I can't wax every bottle myself anymore, so I had to train staff and deal with quality control. I need to scale the business, but I want every bottle hand-done perfectly. It's a challenge to keep standards up as we grow, but we can't let our vision erode. At $50 to $60 per bottle, the hand-made touch is very important.

What advice do you wish someone had told you starting out?

I received the best advice from the beginning, because I asked a lot of questions. My advice is to ask questions and then listen to the input you get, even if you don't like it. For instance, you need to ride around with your distributors and help sell your product. No one else will do as good a job as you will.

From a branding standpoint, my advice is: don't try to be totally different. Just try to be as "you" as you can be. You need to feel excited about it and it has to be a reflection of who you are. At Sonoma County Distilling Company, we're attempting to transform the experience of drinking spirits, and to reflect a genuine approach to the history of distilled spirits—a new legacy steeped in the old ways.

above:

DISTILLERY   DENNING'S POINT DISTILLERY

PACKAGE DESIGN   Megan Keogh, Pixels&Pulp

opposite page:

DISTILLERY   CATHEAD DISTILLERY

PACKAGE DESIGN   Hook USA | artwork by Justin Schultz of The Flying Chair

INDIGENOUS

FRESH PRESSED APPLE
— VODKA —

DISTILLED FROM 100% NEW YORK APPLES

this page:

DISTILLERY   TUTHILLTON SPIRITS

PACKAGE DESIGN   Tuthilltown Spirits

Art Director - Ralph Erenzo

opposite:

DISTILLERY   RHINE HALL

PACKAGE DESIGN   Franklyn

below:
DISTILLERY ...... RAFF DISTILLERIE
PACKAGE DESIGN ...... Auston Design Group

opposite page:
DISTILLERY ...... ASHEVILLE DISTILLING CO.
PACKAGE DESIGN ...... Collaboration

DISTILLERY   COLD HOUSE SPIRITS
PACKAGE DESIGN   Clint Shaw Design

DISTILLERY   SUTHERLAND DISTILLING CO.

PACKAGE DESIGN   Cult Partners

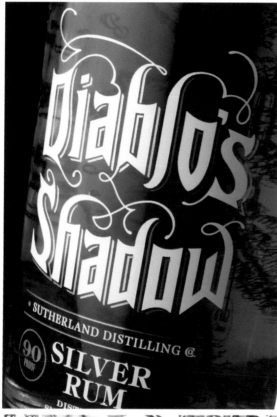

DISTILLERY   CATHEAD DISTILLERY

PACKAGE DESIGN   Hook USA | artwork inspired by Mississippi Delta folk art

GINGER
LIQUEUR

NEW DEAL DISTILLERY
2004
PORTLAND, OR

Ingredients:
Spirits, Agave, Cane Sugar
& Fresh Ginger Root

Produced and Bottled by:
New Deal Distillery
900 SE Salmon
Portland, Oregon

750ml, 25.6% Alc by Vol

NEW DEAL DISTILLERY SPIRITS

DISTILLER'S
WORKSHOP SERIES

NDD

Est 2004

HAND CRAFTED IN PORTLAND, OR

New Deal Distillery

Sugar Cane Juice

Sugar Cane Wash
Slow fermentation
Pot distilled
Unfiltered and

DISTILLED AND BOTTLED

750ml

GOVERNMENT WARNING:
BEVERAGES DURING PREGNANCY
BEVERAGES IMPAIRS YOUR

DISTILLER'S CUT RUM

NDD DISTILLER'S WORKSHOP SERIES | 43% ALCOHOL BY VOLUME

above:

DISTILLERY   New Deal Distillery

PACKAGE DESIGN   Liquid Agency

at left:

DISTILLERY   New Deal Distillery

PACKAGE DESIGN   Allison Arno

|85|

HANSON OF SONOMA

FOUNDER Scott Hanson & Family   **EST.** 2014

SPIRITS VODKA

LOCATION Sonoma, California

PACKAGE DESIGN Stranger & Stranger

Family-owned and operated Hanson of Sonoma is located in the heart of California's wine country, and uses wine grapes to make their organic vodkas. Having leased space to produce and launch their product, the family will open its own distillery facility in the spring of 2015. The distillery will be open to the public.

What inspired you to start a distillery?

Two of our sons were watching the growth of small batch brewers and saw that there was an opportunity for craft distilling to grow in the same way. They approached my wife and me about supporting the project. At first we were hesitant, but the boys did the legwork to prove the viability of the idea to us. Now the whole family is working together in the business.

Tell us about your brand name.

Hanson is our family name. Using the family name is traditional for wine, but not for vodka. We saw this as a way to distinguish ourselves, taking more of a wine approach to vodka that is made in the wine country. Family ownership and production is an important part of our story. We make ours from scratch. Our name conveys who we are and where we are.

Tell us about your journey from the idea of launching a spirits brand to the actual launch. How long did it take to get product ready for sale?

We spent a year and a half trying 155 different formulas using different grape varietals, different distilling processes and different filtering processes before we were happy with the product. We used space in another distillery to do our research and development, and have since built our own distillery. We wanted to prove we had a product the market wanted before we invested in our own equipment.

We live in Marin, California, and had spent a lot of time in the wine country surrounded by world-class grapes. We wanted to do something unique that used this local resource.

Because the grapes we use for our base are seasonal, we have to plan our production for the coming year each harvest. We distill only from organically certified grapes and bulk wine, so availability is limited.

"We also felt it was really important that the label show that we make our vodka by hand. The handcrafted look helps to tell our story, and our story is an important part of promoting our brand.**"**

How did you find a designer to help with branding and packaging design?

We did lots of research in the market, picking up craft and mainstream packages we really liked, finding out who designed them and then looking at their portfolios.

We developed our brand identity and packaging very slowly over a period of time. We had a strong vision of what we wanted and tried three design firms before we landed with Stranger and Stranger. Each firm got us a little closer to what we wanted, but Stranger and Stranger's aesthetic was closest to our own. They really got what we were looking for.

Walk us through the branding and package design process. How did you get from the initial briefing to the finished design?

The design process was very educational. We had a strong idea of what we wanted. We used to live in a house built in 1886, and when we opened up the walls to remodel we found some old medicine bottles. The old medicine bottles inspired us. We also felt it was really important that the label show that we make our vodka by hand. The handcrafted look helps to tell our story, and our story is an important part of promoting our brand.

The first couple of firms showed us their design drafts, and we felt they weren't quite getting there. They did help us move forward, but we're not the kind of people who are satisfied with the first thing we see. Stranger and Stranger's attention to detail and ideas impressed us. We showed them what we'd seen and liked so far, and told them about our concept. We spent a lot of time exploring different options, trying to get it just right. We were actively involved in tweaking and refining.

How did you find the packaging suppliers you work with — closures, labels, glass, etc.?

We researched the top ten suppliers in each category and met with them to see their offerings. We asked lots of questions—my business background taught me to be very thorough. Then we got pricing, and looked for the best combination of quality and price. We couldn't afford a custom bottle, but we found a great stock bottle at Saverglass.

left to right: Chris, Scott, Darren, and Brandon Hanson

What has the feedback from retailers and on-premise accounts been?
The response has been extraordinary. We come from outside the industry, and the response from distributors has been very positive because we bring something unique and different that stands out.

How did you find a distributor?
Our product won some big awards in both the U.S. and Europe. After that, distributors started paying attention to us. We talked to a number of them, including the largest distributor in the U.S., and chose one that was a little smaller based on how we fit into their portfolio, how we felt about their people, and their approach to a small producer. Not every distributor will give much focus to building a new brand. To find one is critical.

What was the biggest challenge you encountered and how did you overcome that challenge?
Managing the sales process. It's very time-consuming, taking at least one of us out into the field with our distributors every day. We had no idea how much time we'd spend working the sales side.

What advice do you have for other distillers starting out?
Take your time and get it right. We've tried not to rush our decisions because we're building a brand and a business we want to last a long time. This new category can feel like the Wild West. You have to make your own way because there isn't really a model you can follow.

Also, remember that you're not just building a business—you're building a brand. All of your decisions must be considered in light of this.

Brad Brunson is Vice President of the Top Series Division at Amorim Cork America. Amorim offers a range of high-quality closures for spirits, from basic to ultra-custom luxury items.

Tell us about the closures available to small producers. Are there stock options they can buy off the shelf?

Almost all of our business is custom. We do have about five stock items on hand—wood and plastic bar tops for standard 18.5 and 21.5 mm openings that are good when someone needs something quick.

We don't keep a lot in the warehouse because cork loses its moisture after 6 months in the warehouse and the quality starts to degrade. We only use natural cork—we don't believe synthetics offer the performance or aesthetic quality we can stand behind. Also, everyone has a different vision of what they want, and they want to apply their branding to their closures, so 98% of what we do is custom.

What is the cost of the stock items, and how long do they take to get?

Black plastic bar tops cost 10 to 15 cents per unit, and wooden bar tops run 30 to 40 cents each. The longer and bigger the cork, the more they cost. Distillers should bear this in mind when selecting their bottle—bigger diameter openings will increase their closure cost.

Stock items can ship the same day or next day. Ship time depends on the location of the distiller and whether they are an existing customer already in our system.

Can stock items have decoration added?

No. Once a closure is made, it can't have decoration added. That calls for a custom job. However, you can add paper or metal stickers or overwraps to stock items, if desired.

What is the process for designing and producing a custom closure?

We have our own production facility in Portugal where we produce our bar tops. Our designer there takes our customer's idea and creates a three-dimensional rendering for the customer to review. Once we're happy with the design, we create a prototype for approval. Then we go into production.

We have four levels of custom closures. The *Classic Value* tier gives the customer the ability to customize the color of the bar top and add their branding. The next level up, our *Premium* closures, allows them to mold the bar top to a custom shape and add dimensional artwork to it. Our two luxury tiers, *Elegance* and *Prestige*, allow truly unique designs using a range of materials including ceramics, wood, metal or metallized plastic, and even precious metals, exotic timber or crystal.

What is the minimum quantity and lead-time required for custom orders?

One thousand units is generally a good minimum for custom bar tops. A price break happens at fifty thousand units. Wood is more cost effective at lower quantities because it doesn't require custom tooling to add dimensional graphics—we work with a partner who can do wood with a custom stain, size, etc. A plastic bar top with dimensional graphics or custom shaping is more expensive because of the cost of the tooling needed for a plastic mold.

The lead-time for this process varies greatly depending on the complexity and uniqueness of the concept. A custom wood or plastic top takes four to six weeks to produce. For the *Elegance* or *Prestige* level of customization, the process can take as long as two years. While they work on these innovative and unique options, our customers can opt to do their first bottling with a plain closure.

Tell us about the application of closures. What equipment is needed for hand application vs. automated or semi-automated application?

Craft distillers usually apply their closures by hand. A dedicated bottling line that applies closures is possible, but expensive. I have seen a small tabletop semi-automatic applicator. And some of our customers get creative and make an event out of bottling, inviting customers to help apply the packaging elements. This works well and creates a sense of ownership for customers.

What are some considerations for on-premise distribution vs. retail? Do bartenders have concerns we should be aware of?

Making your closure relatively fast to remove and re-insert is a good idea. Some bars may take your closure out and insert a speed pour. You really don't need a fast pour for a luxury product, but if your closure is time-consuming to open and close, bartenders are more likely to replace it.

Closures are a key branding element, communicating quality and style to the consumer. They also serve a critical function in preserving the product, preventing leakage and providing tamper-evidence. What are the performance pros and cons of different types of closures?

There are three types of closures for spirits—screwcaps, plastic or natural cork. There are going to be challenges with each type, but we believe cork performs best. It gives a premium communication and protects the product very well. Cork compresses to fill in all the imperfections in the neck of the bottle. Plastic can't do this. Also, cork can expand and contract in sync with the bottle to maintain the seal. If it's applied in a cold room and then shipped to a warm climate, it holds up.

There's a misperception that we run into often: Distillers worry that natural cork will color a white spirits product. We have a proprietary coating for corks that go into white spirits, so this is not a problem. Our cork is very clean, and we supply the same high quality to all of our customers, no matter their size or the price of their product.

Make sure the closures you buy hold together. The weak point in any bar top is the glue point between the top and the cork. We have an R&D department specializing in testing different glues for different climates, materials and application processes. For instance, if you do a wax dip, which warms the closure, or if your bottle goes through a heat shrink tunnel, you need a glue that holds up to heat without weakening.

There are strict requirements for alcohol beverage labeling. While designers experienced in the category will be aware of the rules and how to create exciting designs that comply with regulations, brand owners should also be aware of what is likely to gain approval vs. rejection from the TTB. Langdon Guenther is a Regulatory Specialist with Jim McCoy Alcohol & Tobacco Consultants, LLC. We asked him to share the basics of labeling requirements and the TTB label approval process with us.

What are the requirements for distilled spirits labeling?

The Alcohol and Tobacco Tax and Trade Bureau (TTB) is responsible for all regulatory aspects regarding the distilled spirits industry in the United States. The labeling of these spirits products requires very specific and mandatory information. The following mandatory information must appear on the label:

· The brand name of the product.

· Class and type. The class of the spirit is a broad category. "Whiskey" is one of the classes of spirits. The types of whiskey include bourbon whiskey, rye whiskey, malt whiskey, corn whiskey, Irish whiskey, Scotch whiskey, etc.

· The alcoholic content shown as "alcohol by volume" (ABV). It can also show as the proof of the product. For example, 40% ALC/VOL or 80 PROOF.

· Net contents of the bottle in metric units. The most popular size bottle is 750 ml. Spirits can only be bottled in one of seven sizes: 50 ml, 100 ml, 200 ml, 375 ml, 750 ml, 1 liter and 1.75 liters.

· The name and address of the producer. In the case of imported spirits, the country of origin must appear on the label.

· The federal government health warning statement. By law, this statement is required on all alcoholic beverages containing 0.5% or more alcohol by volume.

· All mandatory information has minimum and maximum type size requirements and rules about where on the package it must appear.

Where can distillers find information about submitting labels for TTB approval?

The required form is available online at http://www.ttb.gov/forms/f510031.pdf. This should be filled out with the requested information and submitted along with images of your labels.

Submission for label approval on TTB Form 5100.31 can be mailed or submitted electronically to TTB's Advertising, Labeling and Formulation Division (ALFD) in Washington, DC. Electronic submission requires the distillery to file an Online Access Request form. The vast majority of label submissions are now submitted electronically because it cuts down on processing time. The recent proliferation of craft distilleries has increased processing time and approval. Five years ago, most label applications were processed within one week or so. As of September, 2014, processing time had increased to 43 days.

What kinds of things can cause a label to be rejected?

A request for label approval can be rejected if any of the mandatory information required on the label is missing. Also, if the Form 5100.31 is not filled out correctly or not signed, this will result in the request being rejected. If a distillery submits a request for a certified organic product and does not submit the required organic certification, this request will be rejected.

If a label is rejected, what is the process for resubmitting with changes, and how long does approval take from that point?

Form 5100.31 can be submitted electronically or mailed to TTB. If an electronic submission is rejected and the necessary changes are made and resubmitted to TTB, this application goes to the top of the application pile. It will probably take two weeks or so for approval of the resubmitted application. Conversely, if a mailed application is corrected and resubmitted to TTB, it goes to the bottom of the application pile and could take months to be approved.

What types images of and language are prohibited on spirits packages?

The TTB will reject a label if it contains language that it considers to be misleading, or images or language that it considers to be indecent. The best reference for Prohibited Practices can be found online at www.ecfr.gov. Search for Electronic Code of Federal Regulations, PART 5—Labeling and Advertising of Distilled Spirits. This section also outlines the restrictions on advertising of distilled spirits — an important subject that distillers should be aware of.

TTB COMPLIANCE AND THE APPROVAL PROCESS

CHALLENGING THE HUMORLESS TTB LABEL APPROVERS

BY MICHAEL SHERWOOD

Sub Rosa Spirits is an Oregon craft distillery producing non-traditional distillates that carry great intensity and flavor. They also have quite an irreverent streak. Owner Michael Sherwood shared with us the story of their (rather amusing) TTB approval journey.

It took over two months to get our labels through the federal maze. They didn't like my wording one bit. It seems it was a bit too mystic and medieval for them. Here are a few examples:

<u>Proposed wording on the Saffron label</u>: "By accepting this elixir, you are now part of the Cadre of Sub Rosa." <u>Rejected</u>: elixirs are ancient medicinal formulas and can't be used in reference to alcohol lest anyone think they can be cured by drinking. I guess they feared the cadre, the insiders who joined my cult, would either heal themselves or maybe just overthrow the government. <u>Compromise</u>: "By accepting this spirit…" changed to "By accepting this bottle…"

They let the wording "Welcome to our fellowship of indulgence" pass with no objection. I guess hedonism is okay.

<u>Proposed wording on the Tarragon label</u>: "Light notes of anise that are herbal and refreshing." <u>Rejected</u>. "Light" connotes light alcohol even though it was talking about a flavor. Can't suggest distilled spirits in the context of strong or light. Guess they missed the 90 proof on the rest of the label. But Lite Beer is fine? <u>Rejected</u>: "Refreshing." You can't use that in conjunction with distilled spirits. It's a health claim! You can use "refreshing" on a beer label, but not a distillate. Who knew?

<u>Proposed wording</u>: "Behind the hidden doors of Sub Rosa lie hidden truths where ethanol alchemy and molecular gastronomy meet." <u>Rejected</u>. Alchemy is the ancient art of not only turning lead into gold, but also concocting medicinal formulas. Can't use that, oh no. <u>Compromise</u>: They finally accepted "ethanol divination" instead of alchemy, but that took them over two weeks to chew on. Thank god I didn't claim you'd be clairvoyant too!

I also had to translate all foreign text used. There is Latin all over the place on the labels. The first two uses of Latin flew by with no hiccups:

Sapre Aude—Dare to Think. Have courage to use your own intelligence.

Quaere verum—Seek the Truth

They have a problem with my use of the Olympic Games' motto of "*Citius, Altius, Fortius,*" which is Latin for "Faster, Higher, Stronger." I use this on the Saffron label and it remains as I designed it. The TTB let this one go, but had many discussions about it. No doubt they feared that the imbiber would think they could actually run faster, jump higher and be stronger by drinking the Saffron infused vodka. Alcohol does do strange things to people, or rather, people do strange things after drinking, so I guess that is a legitimate fear. At least they didn't interpret it to mean that by drinking this "strong" 90 proof spirit you would get "higher, faster."

Evidently there are 100 words you can't use on a liquor label. They can't tell you what they are unless you use them, then you know.

God forbid that anyone distilling alcohol has a sense of humor, much less a subversive bent. Pushing the boundaries of the TTB cost me an extra month and a half and no one got in on the "fun." I should have had these products out by late August. Instead it was the first week of October 2007 by the time everything was printed and labeled. Being a smart-ass has a price. I pleaded my case and had to dumb down the text some on the label. Still, I remain unrepentant.

DISTILLERY   SUB ROSA SPIRITS
PACKAGE DESIGN   Magneto Brand Advertising

PUTTING IT INTO PRACTICE

The launch of any successful brand requires the collaboration of many contributors working to produce something unique and desirable. For a new craft distiller to create a bold and well-defined brand vision—while also persevering through regulatory roadblocks, raising funds and perfecting the recipe—requires dedication. Fortunately, most craft distillers have a pioneering spirit and the desire to create something great.

The craft spirits category has gained tremendous momentum, garnering support from the trade and consumers in a very short period of time. The newness of the category presents both opportunities and challenges.

Information and resources about navigating the process are limited, and as one distiller said, "It's a bit like the Wild West." Everyone is making their own way and figuring it out as they go. An enormous investment of heart, soul, time, money and boundless energy is required to succeed.

We hope that this book will provide a roadmap for the branding and packaging process, helping new and established distillers to navigate unfamiliar territory successfully, ultimately enabling them to bring new and exciting products to market and realize their dreams.

—CYNTHIA STERLING

ABOUT THE AUTHOR

Cynthia Sterling is the founder and creative director of Sterling Creativeworks; a strategy, branding, and packaging agency dedicated to building standout wine and spirits brands. Her firm's naming, positioning and design work has been instrumental in the growth of category leaders. She holds a BFA in graphic design from California College of the Arts.

As a luxury branding professional, she's had the privilege of working with some of today's smartest marketing minds to figure out what makes brands stand out, justify their higher price point, and delight consumers so that they, in turn, share their discovery with friends.

To view more of Cynthia and her team's work, please visit www.sterlingcreativeworks.com

ABOUT THE PHOTOGRAPHER

Alan Campbell is a commercial food and wine photographer based in Sonoma County, California. He has been creating images for wineries and craft food purveyors for the past 24 years. Living in this incredible wine growing region gives him inspiration every time he looks through his lens. While shooting for the wine industry, he began dabbling in home winemaking. He eventually dedicated some time to a commercial vineyard at his home. The "Big Pig" vineyard was established in 2006 and has 4 acres planted in Pinot Noir. Last year he partnered with Craig Strehlow from Keefer Ranch Wines on their own label, Camlow Cellars. You can find more of his work at www.alancampbellphotography.com

CPSIA information can be obtained at www.ICGtesting.com
Printed in the USA
BVIW12n1921100317
478066BV00005B/107

* 9 7 8 0 9 9 1 0 4 3 6 7 5 *